Selling Your Toronto Home

Insider Secrets for Getting Maximum Value in Any Market

Stephanie Wood and Sean Tjia

Selling Your Toronto Home

Published by:
90-Minute Books
Newinformation Inc
302 Martinique Drive
Winter Haven, FL 33884
www.90minutebooks.com

Copyright © 2015, Stephanie Wood and Sean Tjia

Published in the United States of America

ISBN-13: 978-0692437155
ISBN-10: 0692437150

For more information on 90-Minute Books including finding out how you can publish your own lead generating book, visit www.90minutebook.com or call (863) 318-0464

Here's What's Inside…

May, 2015

Toronto is in a booming real estate market. But getting maximum value for your Toronto home is not just a matter of putting a sign in the yard and some fresh daisies in a jar. Even in a strong market, a lot of home sellers make expensive and avoidable mistakes when trying to sell their homes, costing them thousands and thousands of dollars.

For most people, their home is the largest single asset they will probably ever own and most would agree that when selling a several hundred-thousand, if not million-dollar property, it makes sense to get professional insight, right?

We've put together a book on the insider secrets to getting maximum value in any market because, as full-time real estate salespeople, we have seen too many home sellers struggle to sell on their own or simply had an inexperienced or uncaring agent, resulting in the loss of tens of thousands of dollars. We want to give potential home sellers an advantage in the market whether they try to sell on their own, use another agent, or decide to hire us.

Enjoy the book!

We hope it educates you and helps change your way of thinking about how to best showcase your home and encourages you to put the right team in place to help you make the best decisions and get maximum value for your Toronto home.

To Your Success!

Stephanie Wood and Sean Tjia

Why Buyers Love Downtown Toronto

When it comes to the downtown Toronto real estate market, a few key points should be noted. Lifestyles are trending towards more urban living. Buyers want to live, work, and play all in the same neighbourhood. While there are people who are okay with commuting for an hour and a half so they can have an extra 50 square feet of yard, for buyers who love downtown Toronto, it's all about the lifestyle.

People who want to live downtown want the flexibility that living in a large metropolitan city like Toronto provides. A lot of people who live here are jet setters; they like to travel a lot and like to have their social life downtown and not just go to the big box mall on the weekend and get all of their chores done.

Some markets in Toronto are booming. We have a lot of condos in our city and each condo building is about 400 units, so that's a neighbourhood in and of itself. Although it depends on exactly where you live in the Toronto downtown area, pretty much any property that shows really well and is priced right typically won't have a hard time selling.

One of the reasons for Toronto being in such high demand is we're not building any new housing stock. You do see people tearing down houses and building a new house here and there, but for the most part, demand is growing while supply is constrained. You will see new rental apartment buildings being built every so often but the housing market supply is remaining about the same.

Toronto is in such high demand for buyers because we are a live and work city. People want to be able to live and work in the same neighbourhood. A lot of professionals are putting in long hours, and therefore, we don't want to add a long commute onto an already long day.

We want to be able to go to the gym, run home, shower, go out to dinner with our friends, and then go back to work. For a lot of people, being in the city is a dream-come-true environment because our work and play are blended. The city is our lifestyle.

When Is the Right Time to Sell Your Toronto Home?

There are always peak points in the annual market. In Toronto, autumn and spring are the peak points. However, because our inventory changes on a daily basis, the best time to sell is when there are no other homes listed for sale. So you want to list your home when the competition is low.

With peak markets, things sell quickly. But even in slow markets, there are ways and strategies to use to get homes sold so that they don't sit on the market and they do get a lot of money.

Right now, during the writing of this book, the competition is low for most of Toronto. We're always looking for great properties to help sell because a great property is going to sell in any market.

Should You Fix Up Your Home Before Selling?

It depends on why you're selling and what condition the home is in. Because we knew the market was going to be filled with people wanting to come in and renovate, we've told sellers to simply just declutter.

We've told people, "Don't even bother painting because you just don't want to spend any more money than you have to in order to get the most for your property." If it's a first-time buyer and it's a condo that needs a bit of work then, yeah, we're definitely going to tell people to get it ready for sale.

Part of our service to the sellers includes the staging consultation, so a stager will go through and tell them to do this, this, and this. The answer is different for everyone, but before you spend any money, you should talk to a professional.

Why You Should Know Who the Buyer Will Be for Your Home Before You Sell

Before you sell your home, you want to identify who the most obvious buyer is for your market. Are they first-time home buyers? Are they downsizing? Is it the professional who is moving up because now they have two incomes and they're making prime incomes? Knowing who the buyer will be for your home and what those buyers' expectations are is going to help you capitalize on the value of the property.

You'll want to stage the home to get maximum value depending on who the buyer is going to be. A lot of people think they'll just put their house on the market because everything is selling. That's not always the case. You've got two very different people to whom you're selling. One is the person who wants to come in and just unpack and not do a thing—not even paint—and they're willing to pay a premium for not having to do anything.

The other person is the investor who is looking to have to come in and paint or clean up after a tenant or repair scratches or a leaky faucet and they want the house for fifty cents on the dollar. If your house won't meet the needs of the first type of buyer, you should know this before you put your home on the market.

You're catering to one of two markets, and because it's your biggest asset, you want to put your best foot forward and do it right from the beginning.

When it looks like everything is selling, people can often get lazy and think they don't need to do their homework before they sell. Sure, you may get it sold but not necessarily for maximum value, which is what this book is geared for.

How to Find Out What Your Toronto Home Is Worth

Nobody ever knows for sure what their home is worth until they get a serious offer from a buyer to buy the home. However, the best way to determine the home's value is usually by similar homes that have recently sold.

Hopefully, there are great comparables in the neighbourhood that can be used as a gauge. Their home value doesn't have anything to do with what somebody paid for the property.

It doesn't have anything to do with whether or not they've got gold-plated faucets, because unless you're in the business of renovating and selling homes for a profit, you probably shouldn't expect to get money from renovations.

The reason why is that somebody's personal taste is not somebody else's. One person's treasure is another person's trash. When looking at establishing a price to go to market, the best way to go is to establish where market value should be and really heavily market it. If your price is too high, you're going to lose out on people who would be able to afford your home but are afraid that you're not serious or that you're not going to be willing to negotiate.

Setting it high to negotiate down was something that worked great in the 1980s, but it hasn't been working, at least in the Toronto market, for nearly two decades.

When you are pricing it for a fire sale, you take a risk as well. You don't want to be pricing $100,000 below where you should be just to try and get offers because you might not get as much as you could since you're going to be competing with other sellers on the market.

You're going to lose people who are going to believe that you're not serious because they're going to be thinking, "Oh, they underpriced it for a bidding war".

If you see houses that are similar to yours in your neighbourhood going in the $600,000 range, plus or minus $10,000, you're usually safe.

There is more of an art to it than a science and it really takes having somebody who knows how to interpret the information based on what has sold and what didn't sell.

Often sellers overlook researching why homes in their neighbourhood didn't sell. There is always a reason. The market rejected those homes. Why was it? Was it the condition? Was it the price? You need to dig a little and find out more.

Having professionals who go and preview properties every day and know what's happening on the market helps out because they've been inside these homes.

It's also important to know what your current competition is; what other homes are for sale. Get to know the conditions of those properties as well. How many days have they been on the market? It all adds up and tells a story.

All of these little details go into establishing a price. There is a way to test the price as well. We do agent open houses so we can ask people, "What do you think of the price?" The other agents will tell us, "Oh I think you're a little higher." "Why? What's the bargain?" That's helpful as well.

Even though Toronto is a hot market, you can't get $700,000 for a home worth $600,000. Ask yourself, would you pay $700,000 in a $600,000 market?

If it doesn't make sense for you to sell until you've reached a certain number in your mind then don't bother listing your home unless the market is where you need it to be. You will just get frustrated and will end up blaming your agent.

Should You Get an Appraisal On Your Home Before You Go to Sell?

It's really not needed for most homes. With very unique properties we suggest getting an appraisal because sometimes there just aren't very many comparable properties around. However, the value you get depends upon who is doing the appraising. So it can be a bit of a hit or miss. If you're under the five-million mark, an appraisal is probably not needed.

Keep in mind what a home would sell for right now on the open market is different from what a bank is going to lend to you because they're lending money and they're more risk-averse.

What to Do <u>Before</u> You Get Ready to Sell Your Toronto Home

A lot of times, home sellers don't even know what to expect when they go to sell their home. There is a lot of information out there for how to *buy* a home, but you don't see a lot of information on how to best present and *sell* your home. We wanted to share some insights for presenting and marketing your home that you may not have fully considered.

It starts with considering where you are on your mortgage. Have you talked to your mortgage agent to find out whether or not you can take your current mortgage with you or whether or not it's better to break this mortgage? There are a lot of things to consider when getting ready to sell your home that go beyond just getting the house ready to sell.

Have you considered what the penalties are for breaking the mortgage? Have you started to apply for a new mortgage depending upon interest rates? Today, interest rates are at near-record lows. For some people, it makes sense to buy two properties when they sell their house.

We recommend you interview a couple of real estate agents before listing your home, because on the surface, it always looks like they say the same things: "I can get you top dollar in record time with the least amount of stress." Ultimately, you want to look at what's going to be good for your bottom line because everyone has a different way of marketing themselves and their business.

It can seem really alluring to go for a discount or flat fee broker. The only problem with that is that, when someone has been paid up front, their incentive for getting a house sold disappears completely. Also, they might just tell you, "Sure, I think we can get $400,000 for your $350,000 condo" just to appease you and get the listing.

Often, they're just hoping to get calls from buyers that they can take to a different property and make a commission on that sale.

How to Get Maximum Value When You Go to Sell Your Toronto Home

First of all, don't wait until the last minute to get started selling your home. If you want to hit the spring market, don't wait until April 1.

Ideally, get an agent involved at the beginning of the process when you first start thinking about it. They can say, "Look, you're going to need to do this, this, this, and this in order to maximize your home's potential so that we can be ready in a month or two."

Your agent often will have suggestions for repairs or staging and those take time to implement. It's always good to get the opinion of a professional. Some people will want to try and sell on their own and that's okay. Most people usually hire an agent because they want to maximize their home sale.

That's what professionals do. If you want to maximize the home, I would say hire professional help. I know I'm biased because I'm a real estate agent, but I don't do my own taxes. I hire professionals for that because I don't want to learn the tax code.

I might be able to save a few bucks by using an online program, but I'm probably going to lose a couple of thousand dollars because I don't know the right things to do.

A lot of what we suggest home sellers do when they go to sell is to depersonalize it. Take out pictures of family and friends. Because sometimes when people look at those, they're wondering whether they know anybody in the picture because it's such a small world.

Depersonalize it, get rid of all your pictures and de-clutter it. Sometimes all the clutter that people have collected throughout the years actually stops the buyer from seeing the home as if they were going to be living in it. We'll ask them to take out shelving that is extraneous or the knickknacks that are everywhere. You don't need all those little porcelain dolls. Really clear it out so that you've got basic furniture so that anybody coming in can see themselves living there as opposed to stepping into somebody else's home and thinking, "Oh my God, I'm in somebody else's home." Instead, they're thinking, "Oh, I could live here," because they can see the furniture placement.

Some people have religious artifacts around and we would ask them if they could be open to moving them to a different place. This is because sometimes the person walking in isn't going to be of the same belief system as yours. We've seen some places where we've walked into a closet that was actually somebody's temple or shrine.

If they have pets, ideally the owners actually would take the pets and go on vacation for a week during the process when the property is going to be shown and hopefully sold. If you do the marketing right, then you should be able to manage it so that you can have offers on a certain date, but if somebody can't, for whatever reason, go on vacation, then perhaps always have your dog outside. Cats are usually okay because they tend to hide. Take your dog out for a walk when there is a showing or, better yet, have them stay somewhere for a week such as a kennel.

If there is a baby in the home, be extra careful with smells. People like to see nurseries because everything is so cute, but people don't like the smell of sour milk. You want to keep everything as neutral as possible to make it easy for somebody to come in and fall in love with the property.

One of the best things you can do to sell your home for top dollar is to have good photography. You don't have to hire the top person in the world, but ideally, the photography is going to include a floor plan and some panoramas and make it really easy for people to see how fabulous your home is online and want to come see it in person.

I believe 89% of people start their home search online and most of them use an agent for the process of buying a property. You want to make it very attractive online and make it easy for people so they can see, "Oh, the floor plan works," or, "Oh, there isn't a wash room on the main floor but we can add one because there is space."—that type of thing.

The first impression is your best impression. Usually, you can gauge if you're overpriced or if you're not showing well by the amount of showings that you're getting.

The typical rule of thumb is if you've got 10 showings and no offer, you're probably overpriced or you're not showing very well at all. If you don't even get showings or you get one or two showings, that simply isn't enough traffic to attract a buyer. There is something off there. Listen to the feedback from buyers and other agents. They will tell you the truth about what is wrong if you are not getting offers.

If you are only getting a few showings and you think it's priced right, it could be that it doesn't show well. We're creatures of habit; we get used to our own natural habitat so maybe there is something that is putting off buyers.

It might be cooking smells that you're immune to or cat or dog smells that you're immune to which, all of a sudden, other people are noticing and thinking, "Oh, I don't want to have to deal with that."

It could be simple things like there was stuff on the wall and the paint's just not looking very fresh or other deferred maintenance. It could be the price. Because sellers think, "We're going to put my house on the market and people are going to come see it."

Buyers are also seeing five other properties, minimum, along with yours. So your house is in a beauty contest and a price war. A lot of people don't realize it because they're only focused on their house selling rather than on their competition and what is happening in the market.

Why you shouldn't be home for showings...

Although it may feel counter-intuitive, you should not stay home when showings are going on. People don't feel that they can be open and candid when the sellers are home. It puts people on edge. People don't really feel that they can say, "I really don't like jet tubs," because they don't want to hurt the seller's feelings. They're not going to say, "Oh, we think that's atrocious carpet and we would change this and we would change that."

We always advise our clients not to be home when there is a person coming to see the property. They'll be accompanied by a licensed professional who is going to show and sell your property based on their needs, saying, "Look, this is the feature you wanted."

It's really important to allow buyers to have that space to feel comfortable, to imagine themselves and insert themselves into your home rather than you being there and looking over their shoulder. Some sellers think that they're being helpful, but they're really hurting their sale.

Sellers shouldn't assume they know what's important to the buyer. They only know what's important to them as a feature for themselves. A seller might point out, "Look at the awesome jetted tub," but maybe this buyer doesn't like tubs. It's just best not to be there at all.

Does having the seller at home stop a buyer from buying a home? We've actually had that happen. In one particular case, the buyer worried whether or not the sellers were hiding something. They wondered, "Why do they have to be there? Is there something that they are trying to take attention away from? Is there rotting behind the couch that we should know about?"

Because they're not free to explore, they figure there is something the seller is hiding. It's these weird things that you don't think about that are such a big part of the buying process.

By the time you go to sell the property, emotionally you should have packed up a lot of attachment to the property. It should be de-personalized. When you're selling your home, it should almost feel like you are living in a hotel.

What I mean is that buyers want to go in like they're going into a model home sale site so there is nothing personalized there, but there is enough furniture that they can see how they can place things, how they can make spaces work, and how they can make it their own.

If the seller is still emotionally in the home with pictures of relatives and memories of stuff everywhere then they haven't emotionally left, and that's felt by the buyers and will get in the way of your home selling.

Why Pricing Your Toronto Home Is Key to Getting It Sold

Home sellers often have a fear of pricing their home at market value. They think if they price it too low they will leave money on the table. People have a fear of losing out and you don't want to miss out. The truth is that if your property is naturally in the $800,000 range and you priced it at $850,000 thinking that you might settle at $825,000, the danger is that all those people that could afford $825,000 probably aren't even going to take a look at it, as it's above their price range.

When you go online to do a home search, the search bars tend to go up in denominations of $25,000. So by pricing your home higher than market expectations, you could be missing a lot of people who would naturally be able to afford the property due to asking too high to start.

When you price it high, you've missed out on a bunch of people coming into the property to see it and then you've got people thinking that you're probably not going to want to negotiate because it's not worth that amount of money.

What happens is you spend a lot more time on the market than you should and everyone is seeing the house and thinking, "I wonder what is wrong with that property? They've been trying to sell it forever."

You don't want to be that person. That's what happens if you price it too high to begin with. It sits on the market day after day and then you're wondering, "How come? It's worth it." Well, if it was worth it, then it would have been sold within the first three weeks—at least in the Toronto market.

If you don't sell within the first month, there is something that's off. What we do with our clients is if they're really, really scared about pricing it where we know it's likely to sell, then we'll try their price for a two-week period; but if we don't get it sold, then we're automatically going to change the price on this specific date so that we can test the market while it's still alive, before we look like we're stale, so that people don't start wondering what is wrong with the property.

This isn't the best way of pricing a home, but since nobody has a crystal ball, we're willing to give it a shot for very nervous home sellers, this way the homeowner knows they tried to get the higher figure for the home, and if there were no takers, they are still in the safe zone

Anytime somebody is thinking of going to market, we would be looking at a specific market analysis of the competition and even the specific type of unit when selling a condo. We would look at comparables of what's sold and what hasn't sold. It's really tough to be able to compare an apple here with an orange over there in the next condo building if there isn't any market data for it.

Having a good market analysis of what the competition is and having the expectation around what is the "norm" for days on market in that specific house type are key to a successful home sale.

And of course, it comes down to how much competition you are facing. Let's say your market is a condo for sale or one bedroom plus den in King West for $400,000. There might be 30 other people selling the exact same type of product in your area. So price is a key differentiation

But if you list a house for $600,000 in the same area, you might only have one or two of those for sale at one time. The competition for the houses is going to be more extreme than for the condos so there is more demand and less supply. Therefore, the seller can be a little more discerning when it comes to price—to a point, anyway.

Mistakes to Avoid When You Go to Sell Your Toronto Home

Avoid falling for the "Pay us $99 and you'll get on MLS and you'll ride out into the sunset." It's just a bad idea. Anyone that gets paid up front, and for so little, naturally loses incentive to do anything to help sell your home.

When you do hire a professional agent, they're only paid 60–90 days after the actual sale has happened, once it is closed. They'll put in all the work and risk on the front end to make sure that you get it sold and you're happy with the results.

You're not under any obligation to accept an offer if it doesn't make sense for you. With 43,000 agents out there, you want to do yourself a favor and interview a couple of agents and see what they are doing to sell your home. Are they asking what is important to you?

Ideally, I think you'd want somebody who is going to listen to what's important to you. Also, look at what their stats are. Are they selling homes for 95% of the asking price or are they getting consistently more than the asking price for the property? How long are their listings staying on the market? Are they getting the home sold within a few weeks or is it taking them six months, you're locked into a contract, and they're not doing anything? Do they offer a service guarantee? Details like this matter.

Are they promising, "Hire me for $99," and then not doing anything because they want listing inventories so they can attract and show buyers so they can get paid the full amount on the buy side?

There are a lot of things that the public doesn't know about different ways that real estate can be sold or marketed. Ultimately, what sellers should be looking for is what the seller NETs at the end of the transaction.

The NET sheet is something that we go through with all of our clients. It details all the costs—the legal fees, the staging, the real estate fees, and everything else —so that there aren't any surprises because people get hung up on "This is the sales price, this is the commission" and that's it.

There are other factors which contribute to your bottom line and sometimes tax implications as well. You really want to know where you're going to be when all is said and done and all fees are paid.

Another big mistake we see people make is the photography. Don't scrimp with your home photo. We've seen blurry pictures, pictures where the home looks a mess, and pictures where it looks like the agent just whipped out their smartphone and snapped a few photos. We've seen photos taken at odd angles, stretched out, or, the worst, no pictures at all. Whenever there are no pictures, the buyers will just move on to the next house. You're not making it easy for the buyer to want to see your place. Time and effort are valuable commodities nowadays, and if there are no pictures, most potential buyers are just going to take a pass, and you'll never know if they may have been the perfect buyer for your home.

The quality of the pictures correlates to how much traffic you see. Hiring a professional photographer to take these really nice crisp pictures and have the floor plans done is so important in today's market. There are service providers we hire who are professionals in generating floor plans, taking pictures, and putting together a nice video to really capture what is special about your home.

You want to make it easy for the buyer to see your property. This means that if somebody books a showing, you want to get out and make sure that the place is very clean and doesn't have any cooking smells or pet smells. This is another mistake we see.

It's very inconvenient to sell a home. Selling your home is not fun. This is why we coach our clients on what needs to be done, setting the expectations. You don't want to allow only half-hour showings per day, because what the sellers don't know, especially about downtown real estate, is that people are coming usually after work and in the evening to find their dream home.

Allow an hour for your buyer's agent to show the home. There is parking and traffic to be considered. They're finding lock boxes, undoing the lock boxes and getting inside. All of that takes time between showings, so allowing a full hour is helpful.

This way, your buyers don't feel like they have to rush in and rush out of the property. They can take off their shoes, walk around, wonder if that third bedroom works for them or not, and not be stressed out about the time or process.

As a seller, don't you want the most for your money? Then you've got to go to the coffee shop for a couple of hours, but when done right, it's worth it.

How to Negotiate Offers Successfully

Hopefully, if the sellers have done their homework right and chosen the right team to work with, they have more than one offer to consider. There are several things that can happen. The first is that they can accept the offer if everything seems all right—the terms are met, the price is where they want it—then why not go ahead and accept the offer?

If it's a lower-than-desired offer, you can reject it and say, "No, not interested." That usually isn't the best way to go about it, though, because with a first offer, sometimes people are going to try and ask for a discount, because who doesn't. So you might get a low offer, in which case, just counter offer it.

If the first offer doesn't make sense to you, there is no harm in countering it. Don't get emotional about it because it's not a reflection of you. It's not a reflection of the property. It's just a reflection of the buyer and what they've been advised to do by their friends or their family, but hopefully not their agent, but they want to see.

I would always encourage sellers to accept a great offer if they've got one. Don't get greedy like, "Oh, that was fast; maybe we should try and get more money," because they may just walk away. If it's not acceptable then counter back at what works for you, but try not to get greedy over $1,000. Keep the big picture in mind.

Another thing that we have noticed is the curious factor when it's back-and-forth negotiations between the seller and the buyer. They'll get to a point where the difference between the offer price and the asking price is $10,000 and both parties are digging in their heels because of their egos. They don't want to go any further or higher or lower. We call this the *pride factor*. Both agents are working their hardest to explain, "Look Buyer, you can have this place you love it's going to be yours. You can begin your new life in this property."

Or to the Seller: "You can move on to the next chapter in your life with something else instead of waiting around, having people walk through your house or condo some more."

When they dig in their heels, the pride factor comes in; it's almost like they need to be the one who has the last word.

Just split the difference; it's all right. Then you can both be on a fresh start. That pride factor shows up a lot, sometimes fairly frequently.

This ends up costing the sellers money because sometimes buyers just get fed up and walk away. The seller also may lose money simply in costs involved with possibly carrying the property for another one, two, three months. How much more will they have to put in for the mortgage, the maintenance fee, the taxes, and utilities, especially if it's a vacant property? They're losing out by trying for how much more money?

As the seller, it's almost like you have to ask yourself: "Are you a betting person? Do you go to Las Vegas? Would you bet $600,000, just so you can get $5,000?"

Of course you wouldn't who would? Now, if the offer is just plain ridiculous, then don't counter it; let it go. However, if you can work with it and the amounts are very close, then just let your ego or your pride move aside a bit so you can begin a new life by selling your place.

It's also not just $5,000 here or there. There is the also the "pain-in-the-butt" factor of waiting and hoping for another person to agree to buy your property.   , A there is no guarantee there will be another offer, and B) do you want to live like you're living in a hotel? How long do you want to keep the place immaculate?

There is a pride point that creeps up but if you can step back and look at the bigger picture, it may make the most sense to accept the offer so you can move on and get the house sold.

When you have an offer, that's when the market has spoken, and you might just be fortunate enough to get an offer by the first person who sees your property. Someone has to win the lotto, right?

We've seen it happen with house selling; being listed and being sold within four hours. Maybe you'll be lucky enough to get that. Chances are that you're going to have at least 10-12 showings before you get an offer, maybe more

This means that if you don't work with the first offer, the second offer you're likely to get could be after another 10-12 people come to see the property.

Hopefully, it doesn't get stale on the market before that point.

The next offer is usually a little bit less than the first one, because now the potential buyers are thinking, "Well, it's been on the market this long? How come nobody wants it? Maybe they're getting desperate. Let me try a lower offer price."

Why You Should Use an Agent Who Knows In Your Neighbourhood

When you go to sell your home, you should choose an agent who knows in your area. When you're selling real estate, there are two parts to the puzzle.

The seller typically hires an agent who is going to give advice on the staging, get the photography handled, and market the property. Marketing the property is marketing to other agents and marketing it their own buyer pool as well.

The cooperating agent is somebody who works with the buyers and is out looking for your type of property. Their buyer agent knows everything that is important to them and that's why we're getting a showing. That's why your seller's agent may or may not sell it to a buyer that they know.

Chances are they're going to be selling it to another agent who has the buyer. When it comes to niche marketing, a lot of it is marketing. I would say if you're selling a downtown property, then use a downtown agent because they know the neighbourhoods. They know how to sell the neighbourhoods as well as your property.

If you're hiring somebody from a different city like Brampton to sell your Toronto condo, how easy is it going to be for people to get in touch with or communicate or handle offers with somebody who is out of town? It's just not a good idea.

I know we've got email and fax and stuff, but it's not the same as dealing with agents that you typically know in your marketplace.

How to Pick the Right Team to Sell Your Home

You definitely want to interview multiple agents. You want to look at it from the perspective of who you feel is the person who can get your house sold; who's working for you to make sure that that's what their focus is. The agent's focus should be you and your property, instead of just trying to get the listing to get calls for other buyers out there. Are they listening to your needs? Are they listening to what's important to you or are they just selling you on the idea of, "I'm number one and blah, blah, blah."

Ultimately, you want somebody who is going to take the time to listen to you to find out your needs, because we have discovered that sometimes, selling wasn't the best solution. Should you be leasing out the property and buying another one? It depends. There is no one-size-fits-all solution. You want to have somebody who takes time to understand your situation and come up with a plan for you.

We work like consultants, not sales people. We really want to help people and we find the best way to do this is by listening. If you do need to sell, great, we'll get you the best money in the market. If you don't need to sell, that's okay as well. You don't want someone who has hundreds of listings and you're just a number and you definitely don't want to be using someone who just dabbles part-time in real estate where you're an experiment. You want a full-time professional who has the system for getting homes sold all the time.

How to Get Maximum Value When You Go to Sell Your Toronto Home

When we meet with clients for the first time, we arrange to meet at their home because we need to see the property before we can give a fair-value estimation.

We like to find out why it is that you want to sell or how this fits in with your overall plans. Does it make sense for you to sell right now or can you complete your goals without selling it and maybe buying another place?

Ultimately, we want to help people build wealth— not just sell a property. If we see a bigger opportunity for the client, we will discuss it with them even if it means losing out on a short-term sale.

We will take a look at the home and make all of the notes that the house goes through, and that way we'll have an idea when we come back and let you know, "Here is our marketing plan, here is our valuation of what your property should sell for, and here is what work you need to do to get maximum value."

Once we agree that it makes sense to work together, we bring in our staging consultant and we get our photographer to come though and we go through the whole plan together and give you a calendar of events and To Do List

You'll know what is going to happen every step of the way from the first weeks before market, what to expect while we are marketing the home, and what to expect after we find a buyer for you. We give you a whole plan for that. We go through the NET sheet as well to find out what you can expect from the proceeds of the sale.

If you like more details or a no hassle, no obligation home evaluation, get in touch with us, we would love to hear from you:

Call Stephanie and Sean at 647-505-4889 or to email us at info@tjiawood.com.

Here's How to Get Maximum Value When You Go to Sell Your Toronto Home

Ever wonder why some homes manage to sell in a few days, setting new price records, while other homes sit on the market week after week, month after month, and eventually sell for less than they should?

So what are the successful people doing? More importantly, how are they doing it? This is why we wrote this book: to answer these questions and give you an advantage in the real estate market.

We help people just like you get your home sold for the maximum value in any market. A few of the most important selling tools we talk about are our steps for success:

Step 1: We prepare a Strategic Pricing Analysis to help you pinpoint the value of your home in today's market, identify the type of buyer who is looking for your property, and how your home compares to your competition in the market.

Step 2: We do a room-by-room analysis of your property, making experienced recommendations on what to you can do to make your home stand out above the rest.

Step 3: We show you secret marketing strategies used by experts to expose homes to the largest pool of potential buyers, helping you NET the most money possible.

After reading this book, not only will you be light years ahead of the average home seller in your neighbourhood, but you also will want to share this with everyone you know who is thinking of selling their home so they can get most money possible too (after you have sold your house, of course).

If you'd like us to help, just send an email to **info@tjiawood.com** and we will take it from there.